The Ultimate Rabbit Handbook: Everything You Need to Know to Raise a Happy Bunny... and Avoid Getting Ears Full of Carrot Crumbs´

Daria Gałek

Table of Contents

Introduction

Welcome to "The Ultimate Rabbit Handbook: Everything You Need to Know to Raise a Happy Bunny... and Avoid Getting Ears Full of Carrot Crumbs!" - the book about rabbit care that will not only provide you with tons of information, but also make you laugh out loud!

Rabbits are some of the cutest and funniest animals out there, but taking care of them can be a serious business. That's why we've decided to combine the practical knowledge of rabbit care with a healthy dose of humor and wit. Because, let's face it, who wants to read a boring book about bunny hygiene?

In these pages, you'll find everything from bunny basics to tips for training and bonding with your furry friend. We'll cover nutrition, grooming, housing, and health issues, all with a twist of fun and quirkiness.

So, whether you're a seasoned rabbit owner or just thinking of adopting one of these fluffy creatures, grab a carrot and get ready for a wild and hilarious ride through the wonderful world of rabbit care!

Chapter 1: The Bunny Basics

Welcome to the first chapter of our rabbit care book, where we'll cover the bunny basics in a fun and hilarious way! If you're a newbie to the bunny world, this chapter is a must-read. And even if you're an experienced rabbit owner, you might learn a thing or two about these adorable and mischievous creatures.

In this chapter, we'll talk about everything from choosing the right bunny breed to bunny-proofing your home. We'll cover the essentials of bunny diet and give you some tips for keeping your bunny healthy and happy. We'll also delve into the fascinating world of bunny behavior and help you understand what your furry friend is really thinking when they're digging holes in your carpet.

So, grab a carrot (or a piece of lettuce if you're feeling healthy) and get ready to dive into the bunny basics with a smile on your face!

Bunny 101: An Introduction to Rabbits

Welcome to Bunny 101, the ultimate guide to all things rabbit! Whether you're a first-time bunny owner or a seasoned hare-raising expert, there's always more to learn about these furry friends. In this chapter, we'll cover the basics of rabbit care, from choosing the right bunny for you to setting up their perfect habitat.

Let's start with the basics: rabbits are herbivores, which means they eat plant-based foods like hay, fresh vegetables, and pellets.

They have delicate digestive systems, so it's important to feed them a balanced diet and avoid giving them too many treats. A good rule of thumb is to give them a quarter cup of pellets for every four pounds of body weight, along with unlimited access to hay and fresh water.

Next up, let's talk housing. Rabbits need a comfortable and safe place to live, whether that's an indoor pen or an outdoor hutch. Their living space should be roomy enough for them to hop around, with a designated area for eating, sleeping, and playing. Make sure their bedding is soft and absorbent, and clean it regularly to prevent any unpleasant odors.

One important part of rabbit care is socialization. While rabbits may seem like solitary animals, they actually enjoy companionship with other rabbits. If you're only getting one bunny, make sure you spend plenty of time with them and give them lots of toys and activities to keep them entertained. And if you do decide to get two rabbits, make sure they're spayed or neutered to prevent any unwanted litters.

Last but not least, let's talk about rabbit health. Rabbits are prone to a number of health issues, including dental problems and gastrointestinal stasis. Keep an eye on their eating habits and bowel movements, and take them to a vet if you notice any unusual changes. Regular grooming is also important to keep their fur clean and prevent matting.

Now that you have a basic understanding of bunny care, you're ready to start your journey as a rabbit owner. Just remember to give them lots of love, attention, and of course, plenty of fresh veggies! Stay tuned for more bunny adventures in the chapters to come.

The Joy of Chewing: Why Rabbits Love to Nibble

As you may have already noticed, rabbits love to chew. They'll chew on anything they can get their little teeth on - from furniture to shoes, to electrical cords and baseboards. But why do they do it? Is it just because they have nothing else to do, or is there a deeper reason behind this behavior? In this section, we'll take a closer look at why rabbits love to nibble and what you can do to prevent them from destroying your belongings.

First of all, it's important to understand that rabbits are natural chewers. In the wild, they need to constantly gnaw on things to keep their teeth from overgrowing. This is because rabbits' teeth never stop growing, and if they don't wear them down through chewing, they can develop serious dental problems. So, chewing is not just a hobby for rabbits - it's a necessity.

But even domestic rabbits, who don't face the same dental challenges as their wild counterparts, still have a strong urge to chew. Why? Well, for one thing, it's a way for them to relieve stress and anxiety. When a rabbit is feeling nervous or anxious, chewing can help them feel more relaxed and in control. It's also a way for them to explore their environment and keep themselves entertained.

So, if chewing is such an important part of a rabbit's life, what can you do to keep them from destroying your belongings? The first step is to provide them with plenty of appropriate chew toys. This can include things like hay cubes, untreated wooden blocks, and cardboard boxes. These items will not only give your rabbit something to chew on, but they'll also provide mental stimulation and help prevent boredom.

Another important step is to bunny-proof your home. This means removing any items that could be harmful to your rabbit, and making sure that all cords and wires are out of reach. You can also use bitter sprays and other deterrents to discourage your rabbit from chewing on certain items.

It's also important to provide your rabbit with plenty of exercise and mental stimulation. Rabbits who are bored or inactive are more likely to engage in destructive chewing behavior. Make sure your rabbit has plenty of space to run around and play, and consider providing them with puzzles and other enrichment activities.

Finally, remember to be patient with your rabbit. Chewing is a natural and necessary behavior for them, so don't get too upset if they nibble on something they shouldn't. With the right toys, a bunny-proofed home, and plenty of exercise and stimulation, your rabbit can enjoy the joy of chewing without destroying your belongings. So, embrace the joy of chewing, and let your rabbit nibble away to their heart's content!

Grooming, Grooming, Grooming: Keeping Your Bunny Clean and Tidy

Ah, grooming - it's not just for humans! Rabbits are notorious for their meticulous grooming habits, and they take great pride in keeping themselves clean and tidy. But what goes on behind the scenes of a rabbit's grooming routine? Let's take a closer look, and prepare to be amused by their adorable grooming antics!

First and foremost, rabbits are very particular about their fur. They have thick, luxurious coats that require regular attention to stay in top shape. So, just like a supermodel preparing for a red carpet event, rabbits spend a good portion of their day primping and preening their fur to perfection. They'll use their tiny paws to comb through their fur, carefully removing any loose hairs or tangles. They'll also use their teeth to meticulously groom each individual hair, making sure it's clean and smooth. It's like a spa day for bunnies, complete with their very own built-in hair care routine!

But rabbits don't stop at just grooming their fur - oh no, they take it to the next level. They're also avid self-manicurists, and their nails are their pride and joy. Rabbits have long, sharp nails that can easily become overgrown if not properly maintained. So, they'll spend time nibbling and grooming their nails to keep them at the perfect length. It's like a personal nail salon, right in their own little bunny world!

And let's not forget about their ears - those long, floppy ears that are a trademark of many rabbit breeds. Rabbits are very meticulous about keeping their ears clean and free from debris.

They'll use their agile tongues to give their ears a thorough cleaning, making sure they're spotless and ready to impress. It's like a spa day for their ears, complete with a tongue scrub!

But wait, there's more! Rabbits are also known for their grooming rituals with their friends and partners. They'll spend time grooming each other's fur, gently nibbling and licking to remove any dirt or tangles. It's like a mutual grooming session, where they take turns pampering each other. It's a bonding experience that strengthens their social bonds and promotes harmony in their bunny community. It's like a day at the spa with your best friend, but with more fur and cuteness involved!

Now, you might be wondering, what can you do as a bunny parent to help with your rabbit's grooming routine? Well, there are a few things you can do to keep your bunny clean and tidy, while also enjoying the amusement of their grooming antics.

First, make sure your rabbit has a clean and safe living environment. Regularly clean their living space, including their litter box, food and water dishes, and any toys or accessories. This will help prevent dirt and debris from accumulating and keep their fur clean.

Next, provide your rabbit with regular opportunities for exercise and playtime. This will help keep their muscles toned and their fur in good condition. Rabbits who are active and stimulated are more likely to engage in regular grooming behaviors.

Another important aspect of grooming is maintaining your rabbit's nails. Regularly trim your rabbit's nails to prevent them from becoming overgrown and causing discomfort. You can use special rabbit nail clippers or seek the help of a veterinarian or a professional groomer to ensure proper nail care for your bunny.

Additionally, make sure your rabbit has access to fresh water and a healthy diet. A well-hydrated rabbit with a balanced diet will have healthier skin and fur, making their grooming routine more effective.

Lastly, spend time bonding with your rabbit and engaging in gentle grooming behaviors. This can include gently brushing their fur with a rabbit-safe brush or using a damp cloth to wipe their face and ears. You can also trim their nails regularly and check their teeth to ensure they are healthy and free of overgrowth. Not only will this help keep your bunny clean and healthy, but it will also streng then your bond with your furry friend.

Remember, grooming your rabbit is not just about keeping them looking cute and fluffy. It's an important part of their overall health and well-being. Plus, it's a great way to show them how much you care and build a strong relationship.

So, if you're ready to give your bunny the spa treatment they deserve, hop right into this section and let's get grooming! From brushing to trimming to checking teeth, we'll cover everything you need to know to keep your bunny clean and happy.

But be warned, once you start pampering your bunny, they may never want to leave your side!

Binkies and Bunny Flops: Understanding Your Rabbit's Body Language

Have you ever watched your bunny jump and twist mid-air with excitement? That's called a binky! And if you're a rabbit owner, it's essential to understand your furry friend's body language to ensure they're happy and healthy.

Let's start with binkies. A binky is a jump in the air, sometimes with a mid-air twist, that rabbits do when they're happy and excited. Think of it as their way of expressing joy and celebrating life! And trust us, watching a bunny binky is one of the most delightful experiences a rabbit owner can have.

But binkies aren't the only way rabbits communicate through body language. Did you know that a bunny flop is a sign of relaxation and trust? It's when a rabbit flops onto their side, often with their legs stretched out behind them. If your bunny is flopping, it's a sign that they feel safe and comfortable in their surroundings.

Another essential aspect of bunny body language is their ears. A rabbit's ears can tell you a lot about their mood. If their ears are perked up and facing forward, it's a sign that they're interested and curious. On the other hand, if their ears are laid back, it could be a sign of fear or aggression. Understanding your bunny's ear positions can help you know when they're feeling comfortable and when they need some space.

Rabbits also use their tails to communicate. A bunny's tail is usually held upright when they're happy and relaxed. If they tuck their tail between their legs, it could be a sign that they're scared or uncomfortable. And if they thump their tail, it's a warning sign to let you know that they're feeling threatened or annoyed.

One of the most important aspects of bunny body language is their eyes. A rabbit's eyes can convey a lot about their mood and emotions. If their eyes are bright and alert, it's a sign that they're feeling happy and curious. However, if their eyes appear narrow or squinty, it could be a sign of pain or discomfort. Be sure to keep an eye on your bunny's eyes to ensure they're always healthy and comfortable.

In conclusion, understanding your bunny's body language is essential for any rabbit owner. From binkies to bunny flops and ear positions to tail movements, your rabbit is constantly communicating with you through their body language. By taking the time to learn their signals, you can ensure that your bunny is happy, healthy, and comfortable in their home.

Getting to Know Your Rabbit: Tips for Bonding with Your Bunny

Are you ready to take your relationship with your furry friend to the next level? Then it's time to dive into the world of rabbit bonding!

First things first, it's important to understand that every rabbit has their own unique personality. Some may be more outgoing and social, while others may be shy and reserved. It's important to approach each rabbit with patience, respect, and an open mind.

One of the best ways to bond with your bunny is through regular playtime. Rabbits are naturally curious and playful animals, so providing them with stimulating toys and activities can help build a strong bond between you and your bunny. Some great toys for rabbits include cardboard boxes, tunnels, and chew toys.

Another key aspect of bonding with your rabbit is through daily interaction. This can include grooming, feeding, and simply spending time together. Many rabbits enjoy being petted and stroked, but it's important to read your bunny's body language to ensure they are comfortable and happy.

Speaking of body language, understanding your rabbit's nonverbal cues is essential for building a strong bond. As we've discussed in a previous chapter, binkies and bunny flops are both signs of a happy and relaxed rabbit. However, rabbits can also display other behaviors such as teeth chattering or growling when they feel threatened or scared.

It's important to approach your bunny with care and respect, and to never force them to do anything they are uncomfortable with. If your rabbit seems scared or agitated, give them space and time to calm down before attempting to interact with them again.

One great way to build trust with your rabbit is through positive reinforcement. This can include offering treats and rewards for good behavior, such as using a litter box or coming when called. With time and patience, your bunny will come to associate you with positive experiences and will be more likely to seek out your company.

Finally, it's important to remember that bonding with your bunny is a gradual process. Don't be discouraged if your rabbit is initially hesitant or shy around you. With patience, consistency, and lots of love, you can build a strong and rewarding relationship with your furry friend.

So go ahead, grab some treats and toys, and get ready to bond with your bunny like never before!

Adopt Don't Shop: Why Rescuing a Bunny is a Great Idea

Are you considering adding a rabbit to your family? If so, it's important to make the right choice when it comes to getting your new furry friend. While buying a rabbit from a pet store or breeder may seem like the easiest option, adopting a rabbit from a shelter is actually the best choice for several reasons.

First and foremost, adopting a rabbit means giving a loving home to an animal in need. Many rabbits end up in shelters due to their previous owners no longer being able to care for them or losing interest in them. By adopting a rabbit, you're providing a second chance at a happy life for a deserving animal.

In addition, rabbits from shelters are typically already spayed or neutered, which can save you a lot of money and hassle. Spaying or neutering your rabbit is important for their health and can also prevent behavioral issues, such as aggression and spraying.

Another benefit of adopting a rabbit is the opportunity to work with knowledgeable shelter staff who can help match you with the perfect rabbit for your lifestyle and personality. They can also provide helpful tips and advice on rabbit care, which can be especially valuable for first-time rabbit owners.

So, before you rush out to buy a rabbit, consider adopting one from a shelter instead. Not only will you be giving a deserving animal a loving home, but you'll also be saving money and gaining valuable support from experienced shelter staff.

Chapter 2: Rabbit Housing

Are you ready to learn all about bunny real estate? Welcome to Rabbit Housing, where we'll guide you through the ins and outs of creating a comfy and cozy abode for your furry friend. From hutches to indoor pens, we'll cover it all and make sure your rabbit feels right at home. So, grab your hammer and nails (or just your laptop for online shopping) and let's get to building!

Cage vs. Pen: Which is Best for Your Bunny?

Welcome to the cage match of the century - in one corner, we have the cage, and in the other, we have the pen. Which one will come out on top as the best living arrangement for your bunny? Let's take a closer look and find out!

First up, we have the cage. A cage provides a secure and contained space for your bunny to live in. It can be made of wire or plastic and typically has a door for easy access. Cages come in a variety of sizes, from small ones suitable for one bunny to larger ones that can house multiple bunnies. Cages are also easy to clean and can be moved around easily.

On the other side, we have the pen. A pen is a larger, open space that provides more room for your bunny to hop and play around in. Pens can be made of wire or plastic, and some even have a top to keep your bunny from jumping out. Pens are great for bunnies who need more exercise and space to roam around in.

So, which one is better for your bunny? Well, it really depends on your bunny's individual needs and personality. Some bunnies may prefer the coziness and security of a cage, while others may thrive in the larger space of a pen.

If you do decide to go with a cage, it's important to make sure it's big enough for your bunny to move around in comfortably. A good rule of thumb is to have a cage that is at least four times the size of your bunny. You'll also want to make sure your bunny has plenty of things to do, such as toys to play with and areas to hide in.

If you opt for a pen, make sure it's large enough for your bunny to hop and play in. You'll also want to make sure it's safe and secure, with no sharp edges or areas where your bunny could escape. And of course, make sure your bunny has plenty of toys and enrichment activities to keep them busy.

No matter which option you choose, it's important to provide your bunny with a clean and comfortable living space. Make sure to clean the cage or pen regularly, provide fresh food and water, and spend plenty of time bonding with your bunny.

So, in the end, who wins the cage vs. pen match? Well, it's a tie! Both options can be great for your bunny, as long as you provide them with the space and enrichment they need to thrive. So go ahead and choose the option that works best for you and your furry friend!

Creating a Cozy Bunny Burrow: Tips for Making Your Rabbit's Home Comfortable

Welcome to the wonderful world of rabbit housing! In this section, we're going to cover all the tips and tricks for creating a cozy bunny burrow that your furry friend will love to call home.

First things first, let's talk about the importance of creating a comfortable living space for your rabbit. Just like humans, rabbits need a cozy and comfortable space to call their own. This not only helps keep them happy and healthy, but it also helps to minimize stress and anxiety.

When it comes to creating a cozy bunny burrow, there are a few key factors to keep in mind. Let's start with the basics: size and location. Depending on the size of your rabbit, you'll need to provide them with a living space that's big enough to accommodate them comfortably. As a general rule, your rabbit's living area should be at least four times the size of their body.

In terms of location, you'll want to choose a spot that's quiet, comfortable, and safe. Avoid areas that are too hot, too cold, or prone to drafts. You'll also want to make sure the area is free of potential hazards, such as electrical cords or poisonous plants.

Once you've chosen the perfect spot for your rabbit's living space, it's time to get creative! One of the easiest ways to make your rabbit's home cozy and comfortable is to add plenty of soft, cozy bedding. Opt for natural materials like straw, hay, or paper-based bedding. Not only do these materials provide a comfortable sleeping surface for your rabbit, but they also help to absorb any moisture and odor.

Next, let's talk about the importance of providing your rabbit with a variety of enrichment items. This can include things like toys, tunnels, and even cardboard boxes. Not only do these items help to keep your rabbit mentally stimulated and entertained, but they also provide them with a sense of security and comfort.

Another key factor in creating a cozy bunny burrow is ensuring that your rabbit has plenty of space to move around and play. Depending on your rabbit's size and temperament, you may want to consider providing them with a playpen or other form of enclosure. This not only provides them with additional space to move around, but it also helps to prevent them from getting into mischief.

Finally, it's important to remember that every rabbit is unique. While there are certainly some general guidelines to follow when it comes to creating a cozy bunny burrow, it's important to pay attention to your rabbit's individual preferences and needs. Spend time observing your rabbit's behavior and reactions, and adjust their living space accordingly.

With these tips and tricks in mind, you'll be well on your way to creating a cozy and comfortable living space for your beloved bunny. So go ahead and get creative, and don't forget to have fun along the way!

Chew Toys, Hidey-Holes, and Other Bunny Must-Haves

As a bunny parent, you want to make sure that your furry friend has everything they need to live a happy and healthy life. And one important aspect of that is providing them with the right toys and accessories to keep them entertained and engaged.

Chewing is a natural behavior for rabbits, as we've already discussed in a previous chapter. So, it's important to provide them with plenty of safe and appropriate chew toys to keep their teeth healthy and satisfy their need to gnaw.

Some great options for chew toys include natural wood blocks, willow balls, and apple sticks. Avoid toys made from plastic or treated wood, as these can be harmful if ingested.

In addition to chew toys, it's also important to provide your bunny with some cozy hidey-holes to snuggle up in. This can include things like cardboard boxes, tunnels made from PVC pipes, or even a specially-designed bunny castle.

And don't forget about the importance of exercise! Providing your bunny with a playpen or exercise area with plenty of room to run and hop around is crucial for their physical and mental health.

When it comes to bedding and litter, choose options that are safe for rabbits and absorbent enough to keep their living area clean and dry. Aspen shavings, paper-based bedding, and hay can all work well as bedding options, depending on your bunny's preferences and needs.

Finally, it's important to keep your bunny's living space clean and tidy. Regularly cleaning their litter box and bedding, as well as disinfecting their toys and accessories, will help keep your bunny healthy and happy.

So, whether you're setting up a new home for your bunny or just looking to add some new toys and accessories to their existing space, remember to focus on chew toys, hidey-holes, exercise areas, and clean living spaces. Your bunny will thank you!

Bunny-Proofing Your Home: How to Keep Your Rabbit Safe and Happy

Rabbits are curious creatures, and they love to explore their surroundings. As a responsible rabbit owner, it's your job to make sure your home is safe for your furry friend. Bunny-proofing your home is essential to prevent your rabbit from getting hurt or eating something they shouldn't.

Here are some tips for bunny-proofing your home and keeping your rabbit safe and happy:

1. Keep electrical cords out of reach: Rabbits love to chew on things, and electrical cords are no exception. To prevent your rabbit from getting electrocuted, make sure all cords are out of reach or covered with protective tubing.
2. Store chemicals and cleaning products safely: Keep all chemicals and cleaning products out of reach, as they can be toxic to rabbits. Store them in a secure cabinet or on a high shelf.
3. Secure loose objects: Rabbits love to push and move things around. Secure loose objects, such as vases or picture frames, to prevent them from falling and potentially injuring your rabbit.
4. Keep plants out of reach: Many common houseplants

are toxic to rabbits. Keep plants out of reach or switch to rabbit-safe plants such as spider plants, herbs, or wheatgrass.

5. Block off unsafe areas: Block off any areas of your home that may be unsafe for your rabbit to explore, such as the laundry room or garage. Use baby gates or playpens to keep your rabbit in a safe area.

6. Cover or block access to small spaces: Rabbits love to explore small spaces, but they can get stuck or injured in tight areas. Cover or block access to small spaces such as under furniture or behind appliances.

7. Supervise playtime: Always supervise your rabbit during playtime, and make sure they are not getting into anything they shouldn't. Keep an eye on them to prevent accidents.

8. Provide plenty of toys and entertainment: Rabbits need mental and physical stimulation to stay happy and healthy. Provide plenty of toys, such as chew toys, tunnels, and puzzle feeders, to keep them entertained.

By bunny-proofing your home, you can create a safe and happy environment for your rabbit to live in. Remember to supervise your rabbit at all times and provide plenty of toys and stimulation to keep them healthy and happy. With a little effort, you can ensure your rabbit is safe and comfortable in their new home.

The Great Outdoors: How to Build a Bunny Playground in Your Backyard

Are you tired of seeing your furry friend hopping around the same old boring backyard every day? Why not build them a bunny playground! Not only will it provide them with some much-needed exercise, but it will also keep them entertained and mentally stimulated.

The first thing you'll need to do is secure your backyard with a fence. Trust us, your neighbors won't appreciate a rogue bunny hopping into their yard and wreaking havoc on their garden. Once you've fenced in the area, you can start building the playground.

The possibilities are endless when it comes to bunny playgrounds. You can include tunnels for them to run through, wooden platforms for them to climb on, and even a little pool for them to splash around in on hot summer days. Don't forget to add some hiding spots for them to retreat to when they need a break from all the fun and games.

But wait, there's more! You can also add some fun toys to the playground, such as chew toys, balls, and even a miniature obstacle course. Just be sure to supervise your bunny while they play to ensure their safety.

Remember, a happy bunny is a healthy bunny. So, if you have the space and the resources, why not build your furry friend a playground to enjoy? They'll thank you with lots of binkies and bunny kisses!

Chapter 3: Nutrition and Treats

Are you ready to talk about the favorite topic of bunnies (and maybe even humans)? That's right, we're diving into the world of rabbit nutrition and treats!

Now, I know what you might be thinking: "How exciting can food and treats for bunnies really be?" Well, let me tell you, it's more exciting than you think! From the crunch of fresh veggies to the sweetness of a tasty treat, rabbits have a lot to say about what goes into their bellies.

But, as with any diet, it's important to make sure that your bunny is getting the right nutrition to keep them healthy and happy. In this chapter, we'll cover everything from the basics of what rabbits should eat to some creative and fun ways to give them treats. So, let's hop to it!

The Hay Day: Why Hay is Essential to Your Rabbit's Diet

If you're a rabbit owner, you've likely heard the saying "hay is for horses." But the truth is, hay is actually an essential part of a rabbit's diet. Why, you ask? Well, let's dig into the details of the hay day.

First and foremost, hay is an excellent source of fiber, which is vital for a rabbit's digestive health. Rabbits are herbivores, and their digestive systems are designed to break down tough plant material like hay. Without enough fiber in their diet, rabbits can experience digestive issues such as bloating and GI stasis, which can be life-threatening.

Not all hay is created equal, however. The best type of hay for rabbits is grass hay, which includes varieties such as timothy, orchard grass, and brome. These types of hay are low in calories, high in fiber, and provide the necessary roughage for optimal digestive health. Alfalfa hay, on the other hand, is high in protein and calcium, which can be harmful to rabbits if fed in excess.

When selecting hay for your rabbit, it's important to choose high-quality hay that is fresh, green, and free from mold and dust. Hay should be stored in a dry, cool place to prevent spoilage.

So, how much hay should you be feeding your rabbit? A general rule of thumb is to offer your rabbit an amount of hay that's equal to the size of their body. This means that a four-pound rabbit should be offered about four cups of hay per day. It's also important to offer fresh hay daily and to remove any uneaten hay to prevent it from becoming soiled.

In addition to its digestive benefits, hay also provides an important source of mental stimulation and entertainment for rabbits. Rabbits love to chew and dig, and hay provides them with a safe and healthy outlet for these natural behaviors.

All in all, hay is an essential component of a rabbit's diet and overall well-being. By providing your rabbit with high-quality grass hay and plenty of it, you can help ensure their digestive health and happiness. So, let's give a cheer for the hay day!

Herbs for Bunnies: A Natural Way to Keep Your Rabbit Healthy

Rabbits love a varied and natural diet, and incorporating herbs into their meals and snacks can provide a range of health benefits. Not only do many herbs have nutritional value, but they can also aid in digestion, boost the immune system, and even help to calm anxious rabbits. However, not all herbs are safe for bunnies, and it's important to know which ones to choose and how to use them properly. In this section, we'll explore some of the best herbs for rabbits and how to incorporate them into your bunny's diet.

When it comes to introducing herbs into your rabbit's diet, it's important to start slowly and in small amounts. Rabbits have sensitive digestive systems, so introducing too many new foods at once can upset their stomachs.

Here are a few herbs that are safe and beneficial for rabbits to eat:

1. Parsley: This herb is rich in vitamin C and can help freshen your rabbit's breath.
2. Basil: Basil contains antioxidants and has anti-inflammatory properties.
3. Dill: Dill is a good source of calcium and iron, as well as antioxidants.
4. Mint: Mint can help soothe your rabbit's stomach and aid in digestion.
5. Coriander: Coriander is high in vitamin C and can help improve your rabbit's immune system.
6. Rosemary: Rosemary contains antioxidants and can

help improve your rabbit's memory.

When introducing new herbs to your rabbit's diet, make sure to monitor them for any signs of stomach upset or digestive issues. If your rabbit experiences any adverse reactions, stop feeding them the herb and consult with a veterinarian.

You can offer fresh herbs to your rabbit by growing them in a small pot or purchasing them from a local farmer's market or grocery store. Just make sure to wash them thoroughly before feeding them to your bunny.

In addition to offering herbs as a snack, you can also incorporate them into your rabbit's hay or food pellets for added flavor and nutrition.

Overall, herbs can be a healthy and tasty addition to your rabbit's diet. Just make sure to introduce them slowly and in moderation to avoid any digestive issues.

Fresh Veggies for Fluffy: Choosing the Best Vegetables for Your Rabbit

Fresh vegetables are an important part of your rabbit's diet, providing a variety of nutrients and flavors to keep them healthy and happy. When it comes to choosing the best vegetables for your rabbit, it's important to consider both the nutritional value and the safety of the plants.

Leafy greens are a great option for rabbits, as they are low in calories and high in fiber. Some popular choices include kale, spinach, parsley, and cilantro. These greens are also rich in vitamins A and C, which are important for maintaining healthy eyes, skin, and immune system.

Root vegetables like carrots, beets, and parsnips are also a good option, but should be fed in moderation due to their high sugar content. A good rule of thumb is to limit root vegetables to no more than 10% of your rabbit's daily diet.

When choosing vegetables for your rabbit, it's important to avoid those that are high in oxalic acid, such as rhubarb and spinach. Oxalic acid can interfere with calcium absorption, leading to health issues like bladder stones and urinary tract infections.

In addition to leafy greens and root vegetables, your rabbit may also enjoy other types of veggies like bell peppers, zucchini, and broccoli. However, it's important to introduce new foods slowly and in small quantities to avoid upsetting your rabbit's digestive system.

When it comes to feeding vegetables to your rabbit, it's important to offer them fresh and washed thoroughly. Avoid feeding your rabbit vegetables that are wilted or spoiled, as they can cause digestive upset and illness.

In addition to fresh vegetables, you can also offer your rabbit small amounts of fruits as a treat. Good options include apples, strawberries, and bananas. However, fruits should be fed in moderation due to their high sugar content.

Overall, providing your rabbit with a variety of fresh vegetables is an important part of maintaining their health and happiness.

By choosing the right vegetables and offering them in moderation, you can help your bunny stay healthy and satisfied.

Here are some vegetables that are safe for rabbits to eat:

1. Arugula
2. Basil
3. Beet Greens
4. Bell Peppers (red, green, yellow)
5. Bok Choy
6. Broccoli Leaves
7. Brussels Sprouts
8. Carrot Tops (greens)
9. Celery (including leaves)
10. Cilantro
11. Clover
12. Collard Greens
13. Dandelion Greens
14. Endive
15. Escarole
16. Fennel
17. Kale
18. Lettuce (romaine, red or green leaf)
19. Mint
20. Mustard Greens
21. Parsley
22. Radicchio
23. Radish Tops
24. Spinach
25. Watercress

Remember to introduce new foods gradually and in small amounts, as too much of a good thing can cause digestive upset in rabbits. It's also important to wash all vegetables thoroughly before feeding them to your bunny.

Granules Galore: The Pros and Cons of Feeding Your Rabbit Pellets

Pellets are another important component of a rabbit's diet, providing essential vitamins and minerals. However, it is important to choose high-quality pellets that are specifically formulated for rabbits. Avoid pellets that contain fillers like corn, soy, or wheat, as these can be difficult for rabbits to digest and may lead to health problems.

When selecting pellets, look for brands that are made from high-quality ingredients, like Timothy hay, and that are specifically formulated for your rabbit's age and size. Pellets should make up a smaller portion of your rabbit's diet compared to hay and fresh vegetables, with most experts recommending about 1/4 cup of pellets per day for a 5-pound rabbit.

It's important to note that pellets should never be the sole source of your rabbit's diet. Too many pellets can lead to obesity and other health problems. Make sure to also provide plenty of hay and fresh vegetables for a well-rounded diet.

When introducing a new brand of pellets, make sure to do so gradually over a period of several days to avoid upsetting your rabbit's digestive system. And always make sure to provide fresh, clean water along with your rabbit's pellets and other food.

Remember, a healthy and balanced diet is crucial for your rabbit's overall health and well-being, so always consult with your veterinarian for advice on your rabbit's specific dietary needs.

Bunny-Safe Fruits and Treats: A Guide to Healthy Snacks for Your Bunny

As much as we may love spoiling our rabbits with treats, it's important to remember that their main diet should consist of hay and fresh vegetables. However, it's perfectly fine to offer them some healthy and tasty snacks from time to time.

When it comes to fruits, it's best to stick to small portions due to their high sugar content. Some safe options include:

1. Apples - remove the seeds and core and slice into small pieces
2. Bananas - slice into small pieces
3. Blueberries - offer a few at a time as a special treat
4. Strawberries - remove the stems and slice into small pieces
5. Papaya - remove the skin and seeds and slice into small pieces
6. Pineapple - remove the skin and core and slice into small pieces
7. Melon - remove the skin and seeds and slice into small pieces
8. Grapes - remove the stems and slice into small pieces
9. Raspberries - offer a few at a time as a special treat
10. Kiwi - remove the skin and slice into small pieces

It's important to note that not all fruits are safe for rabbits. Avoid feeding them citrus fruits, such as oranges or lemons, as well as grapes that still have seeds in them.

When it comes to treats, there are many options available in pet stores that are specifically designed for rabbits. However, it's important to read the ingredients list and ensure that they are bunny-safe. You can also offer your rabbit small pieces of hay-based treats or homemade treats made with bunny-friendly ingredients.

Remember, treats should be offered in moderation and should never make up a large portion of your rabbit's diet.

Water, Water Everywhere: The Importance of Hydration for Your Bunny

As with any living creature, water is essential for a rabbit's health and well-being. Without enough water, a rabbit can become dehydrated, leading to serious health issues such as bladder problems and digestive issues.

One way to ensure that your rabbit is getting enough water is to provide them with a constant supply of fresh, clean water. This can be done through a water bottle or a water dish. It's important to check and refill the water supply daily, and to clean the water dish or bottle regularly to prevent bacteria buildup.

In addition to providing fresh water, you can also help your rabbit stay hydrated by offering them water-rich foods such as leafy greens and vegetables. This not only helps with hydration but also provides added nutrients to their diet.

It's important to note that not all water sources are created equal. Tap water can contain harmful chemicals such as chlorine and fluoride, which can be harmful to rabbits. It's best to use filtered or bottled water to ensure that your rabbit is drinking clean and safe water.

In conclusion, water is a vital part of your rabbit's diet and should not be overlooked. By providing fresh water and water-rich foods, as well as using safe water sources, you can help ensure your bunny stays healthy and hydrated.

The Latest in Rabbit Cuisine: Carrot Muffins, Dandelion Smoothies, and More!

In recent years, there has been a growing interest in creating homemade rabbit treats and meals that go beyond the traditional hay and vegetable diet. From carrot muffins to dandelion smoothies, there are endless possibilities when it comes to preparing delicious and nutritious meals for your bunny.

One popular trend in rabbit cuisine is using natural, whole food ingredients to create treats and meals that are not only tasty but also provide important nutrients for your bunny's health. Carrots, for example, are a great source of vitamin A and can be used to make carrot muffins or carrot and apple biscuits. Apples, another bunny-safe fruit, can also be used in baking or chopped up and mixed with hay for a crunchy snack.

Other popular ingredients for rabbit treats include herbs like parsley, cilantro, and basil, which can be used to make flavorful homemade herb biscuits or mixed into a fresh salad for your bunny. Dandelion greens, a favorite of many bunnies, can also be used in smoothies or mixed into a salad for a tasty and nutritious treat.

Of course, it's important to remember that rabbits have sensitive digestive systems and should only be given treats in moderation. It's always a good idea to consult with your veterinarian before introducing new foods or treats to your bunny's diet.

With a little creativity and some basic knowledge of rabbit nutrition, you can create delicious and healthy treats and meals that your bunny will love. So why not try your hand at some carrot muffins or dandelion smoothies and see how much your bunny enjoys them?

Chapter 4: Grooming

Are you ready to become a professional rabbit groomer? Whether you're a first-time bunny owner or a seasoned pro, it's important to understand the ins and outs of bunny grooming. From fluffy tails to twitching noses, rabbits are adorable creatures that require regular care to keep them looking and feeling their best. In this chapter, we'll explore the world of bunny grooming and learn all about brushing, trimming, and pampering your furry friend. So grab your bunny brush and let's get started!

Brushing Up on Bunny Fur Care

When it comes to bunny grooming, the fur is definitely the star of the show. A well-groomed rabbit looks and feels great, and it's up to you to make sure your bunny is always looking their best. Here are some tips on brushing up on bunny fur care.

First and foremost, it's important to choose the right brush for your bunny's fur type. If your bunny has short fur, a soft-bristled brush will do the trick. For medium to long fur, a slicker brush or a comb is best. And for very long fur, a wide-toothed comb is essential.

When brushing your bunny, be sure to go slowly and gently. Use a soft touch and start at the head, working your way down the body. Pay special attention to the areas where fur can become matted or tangled, such as behind the ears and under the legs.

If you encounter any mats, use a pair of scissors to carefully cut them out.

In addition to brushing, you may also want to consider giving your bunny a bath from time to time. But be warned: most bunnies do not enjoy getting wet! If you do decide to give your bunny a bath, use a gentle shampoo designed specifically for rabbits, and be sure to keep the water temperature lukewarm.

Another important aspect of bunny fur care is regular nail trimming. Overgrown nails can cause discomfort and even health problems for your bunny, so it's important to keep them trimmed. Use a pair of nail clippers designed specifically for rabbits, and be sure to only trim the very tip of the nail, avoiding the pink area where the blood vessels are.

Last but not least, don't forget to give your bunny plenty of love and attention during grooming sessions. Use this time to bond with your bunny and show them how much you care. And always remember to reward your bunny with a treat or two for good behavior!

In summary, bunny fur care is an important part of keeping your bunny healthy and happy. Choose the right brush, go slow and gentle when brushing, consider occasional baths, keep nails trimmed, and most importantly, use grooming time to bond with your bunny. With these tips in mind, your bunny will be looking and feeling their best in no time!

Nail Trimming 101: How to Keep Your Rabbit's Nails in Check

Trimming your rabbit's nails can be a daunting task, but it's essential for their health and happiness. Here's a step-by-step guide to nail trimming for your bunny:

Step 1: Gather Your Supplies

You will need some nail clippers specifically designed for rabbits, as well as some styptic powder in case you accidentally cut their nail too short and cause bleeding. Make sure you have treats handy to reward your bunny for good behavior.

Step 2: Restrain Your Rabbit

Restrain your rabbit by holding them gently but firmly against your chest or lap. You can also wrap them in a towel or have a second person hold them.

Step 3: Examine the Nail

Take a close look at the nail and identify the quick - the pink part of the nail that contains blood vessels and nerves. It's important not to cut into the quick, as it will be painful for your bunny and can cause bleeding.

Step 4: Clip the Nail

With the clippers, make a quick, clean cut on the nail, being careful to avoid the quick. If you're unsure where the quick is, just clip a small amount at a time until you see a white, chalky center - this means you're getting close to the quick.

Step 5: Treat Your Bunny

Reward your bunny with a treat and lots of praise for good behavior. If you accidentally cut their nail too short and cause bleeding, apply styptic powder to stop the bleeding.

It's important to trim your bunny's nails every 4-6 weeks to prevent overgrowth and discomfort. With practice and patience, nail trimming can become a stress-free part of your grooming routine.

Pro tip: If you're not comfortable with trimming your bunny's nails, a professional groomer or veterinarian can do it for you. Don't be afraid to ask for help!

Bunny Spa Day: Pampering Your Rabbit with a Soothing Bath

Bathing your bunny should only be done on rare occasions, as rabbits are very good at grooming themselves and bathing them too frequently can actually harm their delicate skin and fur. However, there may be situations where your bunny needs a bath, such as if they have become very dirty or have a skin condition that requires it. It's important to remember that rabbits are delicate creatures and need to be handled with care.

Before giving your rabbit a bath, make sure to gather all the necessary supplies. You will need a small tub or basin, mild shampoo, a cup for pouring water, a towel, and a hair dryer on a low setting.

Start by filling the tub or basin with a few inches of lukewarm water. Make sure the water is not too hot or too cold, as rabbits are sensitive to extreme temperatures. Hold your rabbit gently but securely and place them in the water, supporting their body and head.

Using your cup, pour water over your rabbit's body, wetting their fur thoroughly. Be careful to avoid getting water in their ears, nose, or eyes. Next, apply a small amount of mild shampoo to your hands and gently massage it into your rabbit's fur, taking care to avoid their face.

Once your rabbit is lathered up, rinse them off with the cup, making sure to remove all the shampoo from their fur. You may need to repeat this step a few times to ensure that all the shampoo is gone.

Once your rabbit is clean, gently pat them dry with a towel, being careful not to rub their skin too hard. If your rabbit is comfortable with it, you can also use a hair dryer on a low setting to help them dry off. Again, be careful not to direct the air flow directly onto your rabbit's skin.

Remember, not all rabbits enjoy baths and it's important to proceed slowly and with caution. Some rabbits may prefer to clean themselves and may not need regular baths. Always monitor your rabbit during their bath and be ready to stop if they become stressed or uncomfortable.

Overall, with the right approach and a little patience, giving your rabbit a bath can be a fun and bonding experience for both you and your furry friend.

Fur Knots and Mats: How to Deal with Tangled Fur

We all want our bunnies to look their best, but sometimes their fur can become a tangled mess. Don't worry, it happens to the best of us. The good news is that with a little patience and some bunny-friendly tools, you can easily get your bunny's fur looking sleek and smooth once again.

First things first, let's talk about prevention. One of the best ways to prevent fur knots and mats is by regularly brushing your bunny. Use a soft brush or comb, and gently work through their fur from head to toe. Pay special attention to areas that are prone to tangles, like behind the ears and under the chin.

But, even with regular brushing, fur knots and mats can still happen. So, what do you do when you find one? Well, the first rule of dealing with fur knots and mats is to never cut them out with scissors. Not only is it dangerous, but it can also leave your bunny with an unsightly bald spot. Instead, use a specialized fur knot remover tool or a pair of small scissors with rounded tips to carefully work through the knot.

If the knot is particularly stubborn, you may need to enlist the help of a friend or family member to hold your bunny still while you work through it. You can also use a detangler spray or a small amount of coconut oil to help loosen the knot.

Another option is to take your bunny to a professional groomer who has experience working with rabbits. They can safely and effectively remove any knots or mats, and give your bunny a professional grooming session.

Remember, a little bit of preventative care goes a long way when it comes to keeping your bunny's fur in tip-top shape. Regular brushing and grooming can help prevent fur knots and mats from forming, and make your bunny's coat look and feel soft and silky. And, if you do encounter a tangle, take your time and be patient. Your bunny will appreciate the extra care and attention, and their fur will thank you for it.

Chapter 5: Health and Wellness

Are you worried about your bunny's health? Do you want to make sure your furry friend is feeling their best? Then you've come to the right place! In this chapter, we'll be discussing all things related to rabbit health and wellness, from preventing common illnesses to dealing with emergency situations. So sit back, relax, and let's hop to it!

Preventative Care: Tips for Keeping Your Bunny Healthy

Preventative care is an important aspect of keeping your bunny healthy and happy. Just like humans, rabbits can benefit from regular check-ups and preventative measures to avoid potential health issues. Here are some tips to keep your bunny in tip-top shape:

1. Find a Rabbit-Savvy Veterinarian: Not all veterinarians are trained in rabbit care, so it's important to find one who is knowledgeable and experienced in treating rabbits. Ask other rabbit owners for recommendations or do your research to find a qualified veterinarian.

2. Regular Check-Ups: Regular check-ups are important for rabbits to detect any potential health issues before they become serious. Annual check-ups are recommended, but more frequent visits may be necessary for senior rabbits or rabbits with health issues.

3. Proper Nutrition: A balanced and nutritious diet is key

to preventing health issues in rabbits. Make sure your bunny is getting plenty of fresh hay, vegetables, and a high-quality pellet food that is appropriate for their age and weight.

4. Exercise: Regular exercise is important for maintaining your bunny's overall health and preventing obesity. Provide your bunny with plenty of space to run and play, and consider setting up a playpen or agility course for extra stimulation.

5. Good Hygiene: Keeping your bunny's living space clean and sanitary is important to prevent the spread of bacteria and illness. Clean litter boxes and cages regularly, and make sure your bunny has access to fresh water at all times.

By following these tips, you can help prevent potential health issues and keep your bunny happy and healthy for years to come. Remember, preventative care is always easier and less expensive than treating an illness or injury after it occurs.

Common Health Issues in Rabbits: What to Look Out For

Ah, the joys of pet ownership. Sometimes, despite our best efforts, our furry friends still end up with health issues. Rabbits are no exception, and it's important for bunny parents to know what signs to look out for.

One common health issue in rabbits is dental problems. Because their teeth are constantly growing, rabbits need to chew on hay and other tough materials to keep their teeth worn down. If you notice your bunny having trouble eating, drooling excessively, or showing signs of pain, it's possible they have dental problems and should be taken to a veterinarian.

Another health issue to look out for is gastrointestinal stasis, or "GI stasis" for short. This is when a bunny's digestive system slows down or stops altogether, which can be life-threatening if not treated promptly. Symptoms include a loss of appetite, lethargy, and a decrease in bowel movements. If you notice any of these symptoms, take your bunny to the vet right away.

Rabbits are also prone to ear infections, which can cause head tilt and loss of balance. If you notice your bunny tilting their head or stumbling around, it's important to take them to the vet as soon as possible.

And let's not forget about the dreaded "bunny butt." Yes, rabbits can get messy back there due to cecotropes (special droppings that rabbits eat to obtain essential nutrients) getting stuck in their fur. Regular grooming and cleaning can help prevent this issue, but if it does happen, be sure to clean your bunny's bottom and seek veterinary advice if the issue persists.

As with any pet, it's important to keep a close eye on your bunny's health and behavior. If you notice anything out of the ordinary, don't hesitate to seek veterinary advice. Remember, a healthy bunny is a happy bunny!

Finding a Bunny-Savvy Vet: How to Choose the Best Care for Your Rabbit

As a responsible pet owner, finding a veterinarian who is knowledgeable and experienced in treating rabbits is essential for your bunny's health and well-being. Rabbits are unique animals with specific health needs, so it's important to find a vet who understands their anatomy and behavior.

Here are some tips for finding a bunny-savvy vet:

1. Do your research: Look for veterinarians in your area who specialize in exotic animals or have experience treating rabbits. Check their websites, reviews, and social media pages to see if they mention rabbits specifically.
2. Ask for recommendations: Reach out to other rabbit owners in your community or online forums and ask for vet recommendations. Word of mouth is a great way to find a trustworthy and reliable vet.
3. Schedule a consultation: Once you've found a potential vet, schedule a consultation to meet them and ask questions. Find out if they have experience treating rabbits, what their approach to rabbit care is, and if they have any specific recommendations for your bunny.
4. Check their facilities: When you visit the vet's office, take a look around and make sure their facilities are clean, well-maintained, and have appropriate equipment for treating rabbits.
5. Trust your instincts: If you don't feel comfortable with a particular vet, trust your instincts and keep looking.

It's important to find a vet who you feel confident and comfortable with.

By finding a bunny-savvy vet, you can ensure that your rabbit receives the best possible care and treatment for any health issues that may arise. Don't hesitate to do your research and ask questions – your bunny's health is worth it!

Traveling with Your Rabbit: How to Prepare for a Trip with Your Furry Friend

Rabbits are wonderful pets, but they're not always the easiest animals to travel with. However, with a little preparation and some patience, you can take your bunny on the road with you and share new experiences together. In this section, we'll give you some tips and tricks for traveling with your furry friend.

Preparing for the Trip:

Before you hit the road, it's important to make sure you have everything your rabbit will need for the journey. This includes food, water, a comfortable carrier, and any necessary medications. You'll also want to make sure your bunny is up to date on all of their vaccinations and has been examined by a veterinarian to ensure they're healthy enough for travel.

Traveling by Car:

If you're traveling by car, there are a few things you can do to make the trip more comfortable for your rabbit. For example, you can line the carrier with a soft blanket or towel, and provide some toys or treats to keep your bunny occupied. It's also a good idea to take frequent breaks so your rabbit can stretch their legs and use the bathroom.

Flying with Your Rabbit:

If you're planning to fly with your rabbit, there are a few extra steps you'll need to take to prepare. For example, you'll need to make sure your bunny meets the airline's requirements for pet travel, and you may need to purchase a special carrier that fits under the seat. It's also important to make sure your rabbit is comfortable with the carrier before the flight.

Arriving at Your Destination:

Once you've reached your destination, it's important to take some time to help your rabbit acclimate to their new surroundings. This may mean setting up a comfortable and safe space for them to stay in, whether it's a hotel room or a friend's home. Make sure to bring along familiar items from home, such as their favorite toys, bedding, and food, to help them feel more at ease.

It's also important to rabbit-proof the area where your bunny will be staying. This means checking for any potential hazards, such as loose wires or toxic plants, and making sure that your bunny cannot escape. If your bunny is used to free-roaming at home, you may want to consider using a playpen or exercise pen to give them a similar level of freedom while keeping them safe.

During your stay, make sure to stick to your bunny's regular feeding and care routine as much as possible. This will help minimize stress and ensure that your bunny stays healthy and happy. If you need to make any changes to their routine, such as adjusting their feeding schedule, do so gradually to minimize the chances of digestive upset.

With a little preparation and some extra care, traveling with your rabbit can be a fun and rewarding experience for both you and your furry friend.

The Emotional Life of Rabbits: How to Keep Your Bunny Happy

Rabbits are not just cute and fluffy pets, they are also complex beings with emotional lives that need to be nurtured. As social animals, rabbits thrive on companionship, play, and a comfortable living environment. Here are some tips to help keep your bunny happy and emotionally healthy:

1. Provide a bunny buddy: Rabbits are social animals and thrive in the company of another bunny. If you only have one rabbit, consider adopting a second one or socializing your rabbit with other bunnies through supervised playdates.
2. Create a stimulating environment: Rabbits love to play, explore and dig. Create a stimulating environment for your bunny by providing toys, tunnels, and boxes to play in. You can also provide a digging box filled with hay or safe substrate like shredded paper or cardboard.
3. Spend time with your bunny: Rabbits enjoy human company too! Spend time with your bunny each day by petting, grooming, and playing with them. This will help strengthen your bond and keep your bunny

emotionally happy.

4. Provide a comfortable living environment: A comfortable living environment is essential to your bunny's emotional well-being. Make sure their living space is clean, spacious, and comfortable. Provide plenty of soft bedding, hidey-holes, and cozy spots to snuggle.

5. Feed a healthy diet: A healthy diet is essential to your bunny's overall health and happiness. Make sure they have access to fresh hay, a balanced rabbit pellet, and a variety of fresh vegetables and fruits. Avoid overfeeding treats and sugary foods.

By providing a bunny buddy, a stimulating environment, spending time with your bunny, providing a comfortable living environment, and feeding a healthy diet, you can help keep your bunny emotionally happy and healthy.

Chapter 6: Training and Playtime

Welcome to the world of training and playtime with your furry companion! In this chapter, we will dive into the wonderful world of rabbit training and games. Training your rabbit is not only a great way to bond with your pet but also helps to promote good behavior and keeps them mentally stimulated. Plus, playing with your bunny is always a fun time. From litter box training to leash training, we will explore various techniques to help you and your bunny have a great time together. So, let's get started on this adventure of training and playtime!

Litter Box Training: How to Teach Your Rabbit to Use the Toilet

While it may seem like a daunting task, litter box training your rabbit is actually quite achievable with the right techniques and patience. Not only does it make clean-up easier for you, but it also helps your rabbit maintain good hygiene and prevents them from soiling their living space. Here are some tips on how to litter box train your bunny:

1. Choose the Right Litter Box and Litter: You'll want a litter box that is large enough for your rabbit to move around in comfortably, but not too big that they have too much extra space to play around in. For the litter, use a paper-based or compressed wood litter rather than clay or clumping litter, as these can be harmful if ingested.

2. Choose the Right Location: Pick a spot in your rabbit's

living space that they naturally use as a bathroom spot. This could be a corner or a certain area that they tend to gravitate towards.

3. Gradually Introduce the Litter Box: Place the litter box in the chosen location and encourage your rabbit to investigate it. You can sprinkle some hay on top of the litter to make it more enticing.

4. Encourage Use: Whenever you see your rabbit using the litter box, offer them praise and a small treat. This positive reinforcement will encourage them to continue using the box.

5. Repeat and Be Patient: Litter box training can take some time, so be patient and consistent with your efforts. If your rabbit continues to have accidents outside the litter box, don't punish them. Instead, try adjusting the location of the litter box or offering more encouragement and positive reinforcement.

With these tips and a little bit of patience, you can successfully litter box train your rabbit and enjoy a cleaner and happier living space for both you and your furry friend.

Leash Training: Taking Your Bunny for a Walk

Walking your bunny on a leash might seem like a fun idea, but it's important to remember that not all rabbits enjoy being leashed and that using harnesses or collars can actually be dangerous for them. Rabbits have delicate necks and spines, and any sudden pull or tug on a leash could cause serious injury.

Never use a collar or a harness that's designed for a cat or a dog, as these can cause serious harm to your bunny's neck or throat.

It's also important to keep your bunny safe while on a walk. Only take them to secure, fenced areas, and always supervise them closely. Even if your bunny is used to being outside, they can easily become frightened or spooked by unfamiliar sights and sounds. Always be prepared to quickly scoop them up and bring them back inside if they become distressed.

Remember, not all bunnies will enjoy going for walks, and that's okay. Some bunnies may prefer to explore their surroundings on their own terms, in the comfort and safety of their own home. It's important to respect your bunny's individual preferences and always prioritize their safety and well-being.

Hopscotch and Other Bunny Games: How to Teach Your Rabbit Tricks

Rabbits are curious and playful animals, and providing them with mental stimulation and physical activity is crucial for their well-being. In this section, we will explore some fun and easy games to play with your bunny.

One popular game is hopscotch, which can be easily modified for your rabbit. Simply use a piece of cardboard or a small rug to create a hopscotch grid on the floor, and encourage your bunny to hop along with you. You can use a treat to lure them to each square, and reward them for their participation.

Another fun game is hide-and-seek. Rabbits love to explore and investigate, so hiding a treat or toy and watching them hunt for it can be a great source of entertainment for both you and your furry friend.

Teaching your rabbit to come when called is not only a fun game but also a useful command for safety reasons. Start by calling your rabbit by their name and rewarding them with a treat when they come to you. With practice, they will associate their name with a positive experience and come to you when called.

Rabbits also enjoy playing with toys, such as balls, tunnels, and chew toys. Providing a variety of toys and rotating them regularly can keep your bunny engaged and prevent boredom.

It's important to note that rabbits should always be supervised during playtime, especially when playing with toys or in unfamiliar environments. Ensuring a safe and secure area for playtime is essential for your rabbit's safety.

Incorporating games and activities into your rabbit's daily routine can provide them with the mental and physical stimulation they need to stay happy and healthy. So get creative and have fun with your bunny!

Bunny Yoga and Meditation: Relaxing with Your Rabbit

Bunny yoga and meditation are becoming increasingly popular among rabbit owners who want to share the benefits of these practices with their furry friends. Not only can these activities help you bond with your bunny, but they can also provide a great opportunity to relax and de-stress together.

Bunny yoga, also known as rabbit yoga, involves practicing yoga poses while your rabbit is nearby or even sitting on your mat. It's a fun and unique way to incorporate your bunny into your workout routine, and can be a great way to keep both you and your bunny active and healthy.

To get started with bunny yoga, it's important to create a safe and comfortable environment for your bunny. Make sure your space is clear of any potential hazards, such as sharp objects or electrical cords, and that your bunny has access to fresh water and a litter box. It's also important to introduce your bunny to the mat slowly and gently, allowing them to get comfortable with the space before you begin your yoga practice.

Once your bunny is comfortable on the mat, you can start incorporating them into your poses. Some popular poses to try with your bunny include downward dog with your bunny sitting on your back, or bunny bridge pose with your bunny sitting underneath you.

Meditation is another great way to bond with your bunny and help them relax. Rabbits are naturally curious and love to explore their environment, so incorporating calming scents and sounds can help create a soothing atmosphere for your bunny. You can try playing calming music, lighting candles, or using essential oils to create a peaceful atmosphere.

To begin meditating with your bunny, start by finding a quiet space where you and your bunny can relax. Sit on the floor with your bunny nearby, and focus on your breathing. You can even hold your bunny gently while you meditate, feeling their warm and soft fur as you both relax.

Overall, bunny yoga and meditation are great ways to bond with your bunny and promote relaxation and wellness for both of you. Whether you're practicing yoga poses with your bunny or simply meditating together, these activities can help strengthen your relationship and create a calm and peaceful environment in your home.

Chapter 7: Bunny Bonding

Are you ready to take your bunny bonding to the next level? This chapter is all about strengthening your relationship with your furry friend through various methods, including bunny massage, yoga, and meditation. But that's not all - we'll also cover some important tips for introducing your rabbit to other pets and how to bond with a new bunny friend. So grab some hay and get ready to dive into the world of bunny bonding!

Hand-Feeding: Building Trust and Strengthening Your Bond with Your Bunny

You know what they say, the way to a bunny's heart is through its stomach! And that's exactly what we're going to talk about in this section - hand-feeding your bunny.

Feeding your bunny by hand can help build trust and strengthen your bond with your furry friend. It's also a great way to train your bunny to come to you when called.

But before you start feeding your bunny, it's important to make sure you're offering the right foods. Bunnies have delicate digestive systems and not all human foods are safe for them to eat. Stick to fresh veggies and hay as treats, and avoid sugary or fatty foods.

Once you have the right treats, it's time to get started. Start by offering the treat to your bunny near its mouth, but not too close that you accidentally get nibbled on! Over time, you can hold the treat further away from your bunny, encouraging it to come to you.

With a little patience and persistence, hand-feeding can be a fun bonding activity for you and your bunny. Just be sure to wash your hands thoroughly before and after feeding to avoid any potential germs.

Sitting on the Floor: Why It Matters for Bunny Bonding and How to Do It Right

Rabbits are creatures that love to hop and explore, but they also crave companionship and bonding with their humans. One of the best ways to connect with your bunny is to sit on the floor with them at their level. Not only does it make it easier for your bunny to interact with you, but it also shows them that you respect and value their space.

Sitting on the floor with your bunny allows them to approach you on their own terms, and it's a great opportunity for you to observe their behavior and learn more about their unique personalities. You can offer them treats or toys, and let them come to you when they're ready.

But it's important to remember that when sitting on the floor with your bunny, you need to be patient and gentle. Don't make any sudden movements or grab at them, as this can cause them to become fearful or defensive. Instead, let them approach you and make the first move.

When sitting on the floor with your bunny, it's also a good idea to create a safe and comfortable environment for them. Make sure the space is free from any potential hazards or dangers, and provide soft blankets or pillows for them to lounge on.

Overall, sitting on the floor with your bunny is a wonderful way to strengthen your bond and build trust. Just remember to be patient, gentle, and respectful of your bunny's space, and you'll be well on your way to a loving and lasting relationship with your furry friend.

Hands-Off Approach: The Importance of Letting Your Bunny Come to You

If you've ever tried to make friends with a shy bunny, you know that it can be a bit of a challenge. Bunnies are naturally cautious creatures, and they can take a little while to warm up to new people. But with a little patience and the right approach, you can build a strong bond with your bunny that will last a lifetime.

One of the keys to bunny bonding is to let your bunny take the lead. Instead of trying to force your bunny to interact with you, it's important to give your bunny the space and time it needs to feel comfortable around you. This means taking a hands-off approach and letting your bunny come to you.

When you first bring your bunny home, it's a good idea to give it a quiet space to get used to its new surroundings. This could be a spare room, a large cage or pen, or even a sectioned-off area of a larger room. Make sure your bunny has plenty of food, water, and hiding spots, and give it time to explore its new home at its own pace.

Once your bunny has had a chance to settle in, you can start to introduce yourself. Sit quietly near your bunny's hiding spot and talk softly to it. Avoid making any sudden movements or loud noises, as this can startle your bunny and make it feel unsafe.

Over time, your bunny will start to feel more comfortable around you. It may even start to approach you on its own. When this happens, resist the urge to pick up your bunny or try to pet it. Instead, let your bunny sniff you and investigate you at its own pace. This will help to build trust between you and your bunny, and make it more likely that your bunny will want to spend time with you in the future.

Remember, bunny bonding takes time and patience. But with a hands-off approach and a little bit of love, you can build a strong and lasting bond with your bunny that will enrich both of your lives.

Bonding Bunnies: How to Introduce Two Rabbits

Rabbits are social animals and thrive in the company of others. In the wild, they live in groups and have complex social structures. Domestic rabbits are no different - they also need companionship to lead a happy and healthy life. A single rabbit kept alone can suffer from loneliness, boredom, and even depression.

Introducing a second rabbit can provide your bunny with a friend and a playmate, which can greatly improve their quality of life. It's important to note that not all rabbits will get along, so introducing them properly and slowly is crucial. With patience, effort, and the right approach, you can successfully bond two rabbits and create a loving and happy bunny family.

Bonding two bunnies can be a delicate and challenging process, but with patience and the right techniques, it is possible to encourage a strong and loving friendship between them. Here are some tips and tricks for introducing and bonding two bunnies:

1. Choose the right pair: When bonding two bunnies, it is important to choose a pair that is compatible in terms of age, breed, size, and personality. Rabbits of similar ages and breeds tend to get along better, and it's important to make sure that the size difference between the two bunnies is not too great. Additionally, it's important to consider the personalities of both bunnies – if one is dominant and the other is submissive, it may be more challenging to bond them.

2. Neutral territory: When introducing two bunnies, it's important to do so in neutral territory. This means introducing them in a space that neither bunny has claimed as their own, such as a large playpen or a room that neither bunny has spent much time in. This can help to prevent territorial behavior and aggression.

3. Gradual introduction: It's important to introduce the bunnies gradually, starting with short supervised play sessions and gradually increasing the length of time they spend together. This can help them to get used to each other's presence and scent without feeling

overwhelmed or threatened.

4. Use positive reinforcement: When the bunnies are together, it's important to use positive reinforcement to encourage good behavior. This can include giving them treats when they are calm and relaxed around each other, and using a soft and soothing voice to praise them.

5. Monitor their behavior: It's important to closely monitor the behavior of the bunnies during their bonding sessions. Signs of aggression or territorial behavior can include growling, biting, chasing, and thumping their feet. If any of these behaviors occur, it may be necessary to separate the bunnies and try again later.

6. Be patient: Bonding two bunnies can take time, and it's important to be patient and not rush the process. Some bunnies may bond quickly, while others may take weeks or even months to become friends. It's important to keep trying and not give up hope – with time and patience, most bunnies can learn to live happily together.

Bonding two bunnies can be a challenging process, but with the right techniques and plenty of patience, it is possible to encourage a strong and loving friendship between them. By choosing the right pair, introducing them gradually, using positive reinforcement, monitoring their behavior, and being patient, you can help your bunnies to form a strong and lasting bond.

Bonding with Other Pets: How to Safely Introduce Your Bunny to a New Furry Friend

Bonding your bunny with other pets can be a challenging process, but it can also be a rewarding one. Whether you're introducing your bunny to a new dog or cat, or even a guinea pig or hamster, it's important to take things slowly and ensure that everyone involved is safe and comfortable.

Here are some tips for safely introducing your bunny to a new furry friend:

1. Start with scent: Before introducing your bunny to a new pet, start by introducing them to each other's scent. Place the new pet's bedding or a toy that they have played with in your bunny's area, and vice versa. This will help them become familiar with each other's scent before they meet face-to-face.

2. Supervise all interactions: When it's time to introduce your bunny and the new pet, make sure to supervise all interactions closely. Keep them in separate enclosures at first, and gradually allow them to spend more time together as they become more comfortable.

3. Keep the bunny safe: Make sure that your bunny has a safe place to retreat to if they feel uncomfortable or threatened. This could be a hideaway in their enclosure or a separate room altogether.

4. Don't force it: If your bunny and the new pet don't seem to be getting along, don't force them to spend time together. Instead, give them more time to adjust to each

other's presence and try again later.

5. Reward good behavior: When your bunny and the new pet are able to spend time together without any issues, reward them with treats and praise. This will reinforce their good behavior and help them associate positive feelings with each other's presence.

Remember, every pet is different and there's no one-size-fits-all approach to introducing them to each other. But with patience and persistence, you can help your bunny and their new furry friend form a strong and happy bond.

Hoppy Endings: Wrapping Up Your Bunny Care Journey with Love and Care

As we come to the end of this book, we hope you have gained a better understanding of how to care for your beloved bunny. Remember that every rabbit is unique and has its own personality and needs, so don't be afraid to experiment and find what works best for your furry friend.

By providing proper nutrition, housing, exercise, and attention, you can ensure that your bunny lives a happy and healthy life. Whether you're a new bunny parent or have had rabbits for years, always remember to prioritize their well-being and show them the love they deserve.

Thank you for joining us on this journey of bunny care, and we wish you and your furry friend all the best!

I hope this book has helped you become a better bunny parent and brought you and your furry friend even closer together! Now, go give your bunny a big hug and a carrot treat - they deserve it! And remember, if you ever need more advice, just hop on back to this book. We'll always be here to help you and your bunny live your best lives together. Keep calm and bunny on!

FAQ (Frequently Asked Questions)

1. Q: What kind of food should I feed my rabbit?

A: Rabbits should have a diet consisting mainly of hay, fresh vegetables, and a small amount of pellets. Make sure to avoid giving your rabbit sugary or fatty foods, as well as foods that are toxic to rabbits such as avocado, chocolate, and caffeine.

2. Q: How often should I clean my rabbit's cage?

A: It is recommended to clean your rabbit's cage at least once a week, but more often if your rabbit is particularly messy or if the cage is small. This helps to prevent health issues and keep your rabbit's environment clean and comfortable.

3. Q: Can rabbits live outside?

A: While rabbits can technically live outside, it is not recommended as they are sensitive to extreme temperatures and can easily become prey for other animals. If you choose to keep your rabbit outside, make sure they have a safe and secure enclosure with plenty of shelter and protection from the elements.

4. Q: How often should I take my rabbit to the vet?

A: It is recommended to take your rabbit to the vet at least once a year for a checkup and any necessary vaccinations. If you notice any unusual behavior or health issues, it is important to take your rabbit to the vet as soon as possible.

5. Q: Can rabbits be litter box trained?

A: Yes, rabbits can be litter box trained similar to cats. Make sure to use a litter box designed for rabbits and place it in a convenient and accessible location for your rabbit. Consistency and positive reinforcement are key in successfully litter box training your rabbit.

6. Q: Do rabbits need to be spayed or neutered?

A: Yes, spaying or neutering your rabbit is important for their health and well-being. It helps to prevent reproductive cancers and aggressive behavior, as well as reducing the risk of unwanted litters if you have more than one rabbit.

7. Q: Can rabbits be trained to do tricks?

A: Yes, rabbits can be trained to do tricks such as hopping through obstacles or coming when called. Positive reinforcement and patience are important in teaching your rabbit new tricks.

8. Q: How can I tell if my rabbit is sick?

A: Signs of illness in rabbits include a lack of appetite, lethargy, unusual behavior, discharge from the eyes or nose, and changes in stool or urine. If you notice any of these signs or anything else unusual, it is important to take your rabbit to the vet as soon as possible.

9. Q: What kind of diet should I feed my rabbit?

A: A healthy diet for rabbits should consist of fresh hay, fresh vegetables, and a small amount of pellets. It's important to avoid feeding rabbits sugary or starchy foods, as well as anything that could be harmful to their digestive system.

10. Q: How often should I groom my rabbit?

A: The frequency of grooming will depend on the breed of your rabbit, but most rabbits will benefit from a weekly brushing to remove loose fur and prevent hairballs.

11. Q: How do I keep my rabbit's teeth healthy?

A: Rabbits' teeth grow continuously, so it's important to provide them with plenty of things to chew on to keep their teeth worn down. This can include hay, untreated wood, and safe toys.

12. Q: How much exercise does my rabbit need?

A: Rabbits need at least a few hours of exercise outside of their cage each day to stay healthy and happy. This can include supervised playtime in a designated area, or even going for walks on a leash.

13. Q: How can I keep my rabbit cool in hot weather?

A: Rabbits are sensitive to heat, so it's important to keep them cool during hot weather. This can be done by providing plenty of shade, offering frozen treats like fruit or vegetables, and making sure they have access to cool, fresh water.